Original title:
The Ivy That Climbs

Copyright © 2025 Creative Arts Management OÜ
All rights reserved.

Author: Tobias Sterling
ISBN HARDBACK: 978-1-80581-799-4
ISBN PAPERBACK: 978-1-80581-326-2
ISBN EBOOK: 978-1-80581-799-4

United with the Sky

In the garden, up it goes,
A vine with dreams and plenty of woes.
Tickling the clouds, it thinks it's grand,
But it's just a green thing with a sticky hand.

It tangled the mailbox, called it a friend,
Every letter it grabbed, it thought was a trend.
It whispers sweet nothings to bees and birds,
But they roll their eyes like they've heard worse words.

A tiny squirrel tried to make it a seat,
But that furry little chap, he faced defeat.
The vine just giggled and swayed with glee,
While Mr. Squirrel thought it rude, you see.

In the breeze, it dances, thinks it's a star,
But it's just an overgrown piece of bizarre.
As the sun sets down, it waves goodbye,
A leafy little joker, united with the sky!

Reaching Beyond the Ordinary

In the garden there's a twist,
A sneaky plant that can't resist.
It stretches high, it sneezes wide,
With dreams to touch the clouds outside.

It creeps on fences, it climbs on walls,
It sneers at limits, it laughs at calls.
A vine with visions, a vine so bold,
In its leafy world, it breaks the mold.

Green Persuasion

Oh, little vine with sticky toes,
You wiggle up where no one goes.
With charm that's green and a playful grin,
You trap the sun, let the jokes begin!

You wrap around the mailman's bike,
He shakes his head, "Oh what a hike!"
You giggle soft as you make your mark,
A funny dance in the sunny park.

Embracing Sunlight

A happy leaf, a sunny face,
You reach for warmth in every place.
With a twist and a turn, you find your way,
To chase the sun from dawn to play!

You poke your head through window seams,
Inviting in the sun's bright beams.
In every corner, a game you start,
Your leafy laughter is pure art.

Tangled Lines of Destiny

With loops and curls, you take your chance,
A playful twirl in this green dance.
You weave through life with cheeky flair,
Creating mess, but we don't care!

You twist around the gardener's shoe,
With every step, you're laughing too.
In tangled paths, we find delight,
A journey green, from morning till night.

Trellis of Time and Growth

Upon the fence, a plant did peek,
With dreams of height, it found its streak.
Racing up, it brought a grin,
A leafy race, let's all begin!

It tangled up, oh, such a sight,
Confusing birds, oh, what a fright!
A twiggy crown all round its head,
King of the garden, love misread.

Roots Beneath the Surface

In soil deep, where secrets lie,
The roots do dance, beneath the sky.
They wiggle and joke, so sly and spry,
'We're the party, oh my oh my!'

While flowers bloom and bees do hum,
The roots make beats, it's quite the drum.
Underneath, they tap and sway,
A rooty rave, come join and play!

Secret Liaisons of Flora

A bud confessed to a sly old vine,
'I've heard your whispers, they're simply divine!'
They giggled and twined, all grape and green,
'In leafy romance, we reign supreme!'

The daisies watched, with eyes quite wide,
'Oh dear, more drama!' they sighed with pride.
While Sedge clutched Moss, in thick delight,
'Let's not get caught in their leafy plight!'

Flourish in Unlikely Places

A daring sprout peeks through the cracks,
'Look at me! I've got no knack!'
On pavement, it winks, in sunshine's grace,
'Who knew the street was my perfect space?'

Then dandelions joined the dance,
Who knew that weeds could take a chance?
With roots so bold, they claim their place,
In urban jungles, they find their lace!

Buds of Resilience

In the garden where laughter plays,
Tiny buds dance in sunny rays.
With a wiggle and a twist, they try,
To grow up high, oh me, oh my!

Chasing shadows, bold and bright,
They giggle as they start their flight.
With roots that tickle and stems that tease,
They climb up fences with the greatest of ease.

Battling Gravity's Grip

Leaves that tussle, oh what a sight,
Trying to soar, but stuck in plight.
With a jiggle and jump, they fight the force,
While laughing at the ants, a comical course.

Swinging on tendrils, they slip and slide,
Waving at birds that swoop and glide.
In a world of green, they make it fun,
Chasing the sun, oh what a run!

Stories Written in Green

Every leaf whispers tales untold,
Of windy adventures, both bold and cold.
They chortle with frogs in a gentle brook,
A saga of sprouts, everyone's overlooked.

Bouncing off branches, giggles echo clear,
The stories unfold from the top of the sphere.
In a world of green, where laughter gleams,
Every vine's a bard, weaving leafy dreams.

A Symphony of Climbing Leaves

In the springtime air, the leaves rehearse,
With every twist, they sing a verse.
Playing tag with the breeze, a merry jig,
In their leafy coats, they dance and dig.

From garden walls to tallest trees,
They create a tune that floats on the breeze.
With a flip and a flap, they take a bow,
A symphony of green, oh look at them now!

Landscapes of the Heart Unfurled

In gardens where chaos does reign,
A vine took a trip on a train.
It slipped on a seat, oh what a sight,
The passengers laughed at its flight.

With curls like a jester's big hat,
It climbed up the wall, patted a cat.
The cat gave a glance, then wandered away,
While the vine claimed the couch for its stay.

Sunbathing on driveways at noon,
It tried to serenade a raccoon.
The raccoon just rolled its eyes in disdain,
As the vine sought to start a rock band campaign.

A twist here, a turn there, oh what a show,
This green little prankster steals all the glow.
In gardens, it dances, no worry, no fear,
For life as a vine is divinely sincere.

Their Unseen Pathways

Through cracks in the pavement it wanders,
Not caring for policies of trespassers.
With each tiny step, it makes its plea,
"Oh look at me, won't you set me free?"

A noodle of green on an endless quest,
Plotting and scheming to claim the best.
It tugged at a fence, made it sway,
The homeowner grumbled, "Not today!"

It sneaks 'round the garden, a sly little trick,
Hitching a ride with a dog named Mick.
Chasing butterflies, dancing in the breeze,
Making a ruckus, with so much ease.

With roots deep in laughter, it's nourished with glee,
Plotting its route with a smirk of esprit.
A leafy comedian on pathways unfurled,
Turning the mundane into something absurd.

Tendrils of Aspiration

In a corner of dusk, where dreams take flight,
Lurks a vine with ambitions, ready to bite.
It reaches for stars with a twist and a twang,
Hoping to catch a note that it sang.

On a trellis it dreams it's a top-tier climb,
Curling through life, one root at a time.
Each tendril a story, each leaf a cheer,
Befriending the shadows, spreading good cheer.

It's tangled with laughter and spruced with delight,
Pressing its luck, but never too tight.
Its goal is quite clear: to dance in the sun,
And wear all the mischief like a silk bun.

Through the garden it wobbles, all winks and wiggles,
While sneaky reflections do silly giggles.
With every new inch, it's a party inside,
For vines with ambition do nothing but glide.

Whispering Vines

In the quiet of night, where fantasies grow,
The vines have confessions, oh don't you know?
They whisper sweet secrets into the breeze,
Of all of their mischief beneath the tall trees.

Their leaves tell of parties, both wild and loud,
As tendrils entwine behind bushes, proud.
A flower spills secrets, a rose in the dark,
Of a daring escapade sparked by a lark.

With giggles and rustles, the night softly hums,
As the vines roll around, making all sorts of puns.
Each twist and each turn, such a jolly design,
Spinning tall tales like a well-aged wine.

Under the moonlight, they laugh and they sway,
A jester's parade in their leafy array.
For in the stillness, their laughter does soar,
And whispering vines are forever more.

Climbing Through Forgotten Walls

Beneath the crumbling bricks we find,
A little greenery, quite unconfined.
Peeking through the cracks, it grins so wide,
Making sure no secret's left to hide.

With each new twist, it plays a game,
Pretending it knows all the names.
The stubborn roots, they laugh with glee,
As if they own the whole marquee.

Funny how it clings without a care,
Scaling heights, not wishing to beware.
The walls might crumble, but it won't budge,
Just finding humor in every grudge.

So long as sunbeams dance above,
It frolics freely, like a dove.
Who knew such folly could be so tall?
The punchline found in a leafy sprawl.

Tracery of Ambition

Winding upward, oh so spry,
With dreams of reaching the open sky.
A wild one, always aiming high,
Hoping that one day it can fly.

It doodles patterns on the wall,
As if it's planning a grand ball.
Each leaf a step in a silly dance,
Turning every glance into a chance.

Friends cheer on the daring climb,
With roots that scribble their own rhyme.
"Look at me!" it jokes with flair,
As the wind tosses about its hair.

Though ambition may seem quite absurd,
It chuckles at each tiny word.
For in the silliness, it has found,
The secret laughter of the ground.

Spirals of Unseen Dreams

Curling in circles, oh, what a sight,
Dreaming of soaring in the moonlight.
It twists and twirls with such delight,
Making shadows dance in the night.

Whispers of wishes tucked in each vine,
Telling tales of its silly design.
With a chuckle, it plans a surprise,
To spring forth laughter before our eyes.

Who knew ambition could be this fun,
A playful spirit under the sun?
It giggles softly, embracing the climb,
In spirals of nonsense, lost in time.

So dare to dream, as the leaves do tease,
In winding stories that never cease.
For laughter grows when the roots entwine,
And joy can flourish in every line.

Grasping for Sunlight

Reaching for rays with a cheeky grin,
Pulling the clouds into the spin.
In a race to catch that golden gleam,
It pokes and prods, like it's in a dream.

"Catch me if you can!" it shouts with glee,
Flirting with sunshine, oh, let it be!
It's a game of hide and seek, oh so bright,
Chasing the day, with all its might.

Despite the odds, it doesn't despair,
Stretching its limbs in the sunny air.
With roots entwined, it gathers cheer,
And somehow makes the clouds disappear.

Through squeaks and giggles, it finds its way,
Claiming the spotlight, come what may.
For in the dance of life so spry,
Who knew a flower could be so sly?

Hidden Pathways in Green

In corners where shadows twist and turn,
A sneaky vine plots for its chance to learn.
It tiptoes up fences, wave goodbye,
Saying, "I'm just here for a little sky!"

With leaves that tickle as they sway,
It mischiefs about in the sun's warm play.
Each branch a voyager, a proper tease,
Climbing higher with every little breeze.

A lizard grins on a leafy throne,
This green guest makes its house a home.
The garden giggles, can't hold its cheer,
As creepers sway and whisper, "We're in gear!"

Winding through blooms, it hums a tune,
"I'm here to party under the moon!"
With every twist, it takes a chance,
In this wild world of nature's dance.

The Climbing Dance

In a race against time, a vine takes flight,
It's the acrobat of the garden, what a sight!
With each tiny tendril, it reaches out,
Saying, "Watch me go!" with a happy shout.

It climbs the wall with a playful flick,
A verdant lass doing her best trick.
Neighboring flowers giggle and sway,
"Keep going, you woozy green cabaret!"

Up above, the sun gives a wink,
As the climbing vine makes the birds think.
Giggling petals whisper in delight,
"Can we join in this wild, leafy flight?"

Among the branches, the fun never ends,
As the wily vine plays with all its friends.
Nature's own jester, such a grand romance,
In the lush garden, they all join the dance.

Vertical Embrace of Nature

A goofy green fellow with a cheeky grin,
Decided to wear the bark like skin.
"I'm just embracing my tree friend tight!"
It chuckled aloud, what a silly sight.

Waltzing up trunks without a care,
In a leafy hug, it finds its flair.
"You cannot resist my charm, oh dear!"
Nature's own comedian, let's give a cheer!

The squirrels pause in their nutty plight,
Staring at this vine's curious height.
With each tendril stretching to the blue,
It's as if they're dancing, this merry crew!

And so it climbs, with a jump and a spin,
Not a moment lost, this green little twin.
From roots to the sky, it takes its chance,
In nature's embrace, it loves to prance!

Seeking the Sun's Caress

With a splash of green and a touch of glee,
A little climber shouts, "Look at me!"
It stretches out, yearning for light,
Dancing along in a merry flight.

From fence to wall, it hops and skips,
Taking wild turns, no time for slips.
"Where's that sun? Oh, let me run!
To kiss its warmth, this will be fun!"

The daisies laugh, encouraging views,
While the ivy tries out some funky moves.
It twists and twirls, a flourish with flair,
Hoping for the sun's gracious care.

In a world of green, it finds its way,
Charting a course for that sunny ray.
Witty and spry, it makes its quest,
For the glowing touch that's simply the best!

Embrace of Green Shadows

In the garden, green things creep,
They wiggle and they twist, oh so neat.
They climb up walls with all their might,
Whispering secrets in the night.

Little tendrils reach for fate,
Tickling bricks, they think it's great!
A race to the top, oh what a sight,
Even the moon is feeling light.

They hug the fences like an old friend,
Taking a break, is that the end?
With each new inch, they laugh and cheer,
"Look out world, we're almost here!"

Spreading joy with every loop,
Stumbling through like a clumsy troop.
In their leafy, green ballet,
Dancing on walls, come what may.

Ascending Dreams

Reaching high, a leafy spree,
Poking fun at gravity!
With each stretch, they twist and shout,
"Hey there, world, we're climbing out!"

Bouncing up with silly glee,
They tease the birds, "Come race with me!"
Caught in hair, they giggle loud,
Among the branches, feeling proud.

Tangled up in a leafy mix,
Funny faces, nature's tricks.
In every nook, they plot and scheme,
Climbing high to chase their dream.

A grand parade of green delight,
Whirling 'round in the morning light.
So here's to those who reach so high,
With dreams that stretch beyond the sky!

Nature's Silent Ascension

Quietly creeping, never a rush,
Sipping sunlight, in a lush hush.
Patience of green, they snicker sly,
"Up we go, oh me, oh my!"

Climbing trees with clumsy grace,
Bumping into every space.
"Oh watch me now, I'm growing tall!"
"Oops, my dear, I've hit a wall!"

Like sneaky socks in a laundry game,
They snag on branches, oh what a shame!
But laughing hard, they keep on climbing,
Nature's jesters, always rhyming!

So here they go, with leafy flair,
Scaling heights with vivid care.
In this green race, one thing is true,
Life is better when shared with a crew!

Grasping for the Sky

With fingertips of green delight,
They poke at clouds, oh what a sight!
"Excuse me, sun! Can we borrow rays?"
Sneaky vines with silly ways.

Scaling heights like daring fools,
Wobbling in nature's schools.
Branch to branch, they giggle and sway,
"Just a bit higher, hip-hip-hooray!"

Tickling leaves, they make a fuss,
Racing shadows, who's in a rush?
In this green game, who holds the crown?
"Up we go, till we topple down!"

So let them climb, with laughter loud,
Conquering heights, oh how they're proud!
In every twist, in every flip,
Life's a journey, let it rip!

Leap of Nature

In the garden, a green spree,
A plant doing yoga, what a sight to see!
With each twist and a cheeky bend,
It stretches high, it's no trend.

The flowers gasp at its daring pose,
As it climbs the fence, oh how it grows!
"Watch me stretch and reach the sky!"
Says the cheeky plant passing by.

A race with the beetles, who is the best?
They've got legs, but it's got zest!
With every inch under the sun,
It laughs, saying, "I'm just having fun!"

So if you're feeling a little down,
Just be like the plant, wear that crown!
Climb up high, don't be shy,
In this wild garden, let laughter fly.

Flourishing Against All Odds

Tiny sprout in a crack of stone,
Who knew petals could be so prone?
Fighting through breaks with all its might,
A true champion, ready for a fight.

"Hey, look at me!" it boasts with pride,
Poking through cracks, it won't hide.
While the daisies roll their eyes,
It just laughs, reaching for the skies.

Its friends the weeds, they cheer it on,
"Let's show the world that we belong!"
With roots so strong, they hold it tight,
A vine going rogue, causing delight.

Who needs a garden when you've got grit?
This sprout with sass won't ever quit!
So let's take a lesson from this show,
Against all odds, just watch it grow!

Reaching New Horizons

A mischievous vine on a quest for height,
Wandering wildly under the moonlight.
With dreams of the roof and the top of the wall,
It says, "Catch me if you can!" to all.

Bouncing off fences, it wiggles with glee,
"My leafy ambitions, just wait and see!"
As it creeps past the porch, oh what a thrill,
A climber's delight, it's got the skill.

It tickles the cat, who jumps with surprise,
While birds take selfies with glistening eyes.
"Look at our friend, such a wild ride!
Reaching for the stars, come join the ride!"

A tangle of fun, what a playful mess,
Who knew climbing could be such a stress?
With laughter and joy, let's clamber and sway,
For this vine's adventure is here to stay!

A Struggle for Sunlight

In the battle for light, what a scene,
Plants in a line, each one looks keen.
"Step aside, I need that beam!"
Said one green friend, plotting a scheme.

Leaves rustle softly with whispers of haste,
As shadows shift, there's no time to waste.
"Move over, I promise I won't bite!"
A dance in the garden, such a funny sight.

The tallest blooms, acting all grand,
Pretending they'll share, what a plan!
But the cheeky little sprouts, standing so bold,
Say, "We'll take this sun, if truth be told!"

And in this light-hearted, leafy fray,
They sway and giggle in a sunny ballet.
Each plant with a story, and all in good fun,
Competing for glory, let the games run!

From Earth to the Skies

In a garden bustling with glee,
A plant found a ladder, you see!
It climbed up a fence, in a rush,
Saying, "Look at me, I'm a bush!"

It tickled the clouds with its leaves,
While giggling, it danced with the breeze.
"I just want a selfie up here!"
Shouted, hoping the neighbors would cheer!

A bird perched and said, "What a view!"
The plant blushed, saying, "Thanks, how do you?"
As it waved its green arms below,
Other plants said, "Hey, let's go!"

But back on the ground, they would sigh,
Stuck in the dirt, no way to fly.
Yet up in the air, how it beams!
Dancing and laughing, fulfilling its dreams!

Trails of Persistent Green

There's a vine that thinks it can run,
Wraps around houses, oh what fun!
"I'll reach for the stars, just you wait,"
Said the vine on a fence, feeling great.

Neighbors call it the 'green monster',
Chasing down squirrels like a sponsor.
"I can climb faster than you!"
Challenging everything that moves, it's true!

Its leaves wave like flags in a race,
With a smile that puts grass in its place.
"Look at me go!" it proudly proclaims,
While the daisies shake heads, calling it names!

Yet, deep down, it just wants to play,
To tickle the skies, come what may!
Irony thick in its leafy hum,
To stretch and grow tall, a true plant bum!

Ascendant Whispers

Up from the ground, it took flight,
Climbing higher with delight!
"I'm on a mission, can't you see?"
"To touch the stars, just wait for me!"

Neighbors point and laugh quite loud,
"That plant thinks it's a part of the crowd!"
While the sun shines, it stretches wide,
Swaying with the wind, it filled with pride.

"Is that a bird? No, just me!"
It twirls like a dancer, oh what a spree!
With every green inch, it shows its flair,
Chasing down dreams, hanging in air!

Whispers of leaves in a joyful tune,
Thinking it's destined to meet the moon.
While roots stay grounded, arms reach true,
A plant with ambitions, for skies it flew!

Grasping the Horizon

With tendrils outstretched, it leads the way,
Searching for fun, where the sunlight plays.
"I'm more than just leaves, I'm a star!"
Said the vine, reaching out from afar.

"Excuse me, fence! You've guarded too long,
Let me slide over, I've got a song!"
It wriggled and giggled, a climb on repeat,
The gardener laughed, stepping on its feet.

It tangled with flowers, in joyous delight,
"I'm here for the party, let's dance tonight!"
It took a few spins, with a hop and a cheer,
While petals rolled their eyes, yet stayed near.

And in the moonlight, it finally felt free,
Whispering secrets to the old oak tree.
"I just want to play, don't hold me down!"
A vine with a dream, and a comical frown!

Revelations in Every Leaf

Upon the wall, green whispers sway,
"Life is grand!" they seem to say.
Lost my shoe? Well, not to fret,
I've found a treasure, you can bet!

This leafy chatter holds the key,
To giggles shared, from me to thee.
I peered too close, took quite a risk,
Caught by a flower, it's quite the brisk!

What secrets lie in tangled vines?
Perhaps they laugh at our designs.
With every twist, they tease and play,
Reminding us to seize the day!

So here I stand, a leaf-bound fool,
Taking notes from nature's school.
Laughter sprouts where ivy weaves,
And life is wild among the leaves!

Spirited Spirals of Hope

In spirals bright, the green things grow,
Peppering stones, a dazzling show.
Dancing shadows twirl in fun,
Who knew we'd share our day in sun?

They cling and climb, no fear of fall,
While I trip over a garden wall.
Waving goodbyes to all my woes,
I find my fate among the rows!

With giggles captured in each twist,
Life's little quirks can't be missed.
They grin with glee, a lively scope,
Teaching us all to dare and hope!

Oh, to be like those sprightly greens,
To stretch and flex in their routines!
In every curve, a merry play,
Embracing joy the ivy way!

Flourish Amidst the Stone

In cracks of stone, they boldly bloom,
Whispers of joy dispel the gloom.
A dance of green amidst the gray,
Making every frown decay!

Who knew that moss could crack a joke?
Underneath, the laughter stokes.
With every crack, they slyly sneak,
Growing taller, louder than you'd think!

The stones stand firm, yet so outclassed,
As leafy jokers slowly amassed.
In tangled laughter, they're our guide,
Flourishing with playful pride!

From merry roots to sunny skies,
They teach us how to modernize.
So next time you walk down a lane,
Remember those who cause the gain!

Hidden Lives on Worn Surfaces

Upon the fence, a world unfolds,
With tales untold and laughs of gold.
Creeping tales of little gnomes,
On painted posts, they make their homes!

Amidst the cracks, they hide with glee,
Painting smiles for all to see.
What joys await in every crevice?
A secret life, oh, how they relish!

So peek a little closer now,
To find the fun, we'll make a vow.
In every inch, a tiny jest,
Nature's knock-knock—it's quite the quest!

So let the weeds and mosses thrive,
In every space, they've come alive.
With laughter shared, we'll find our place,
In worn-out worlds, we'll leave a trace!

Life in Layers of Green

In the garden, green and spry,
A little plant gives it a try.
With leaves like arms, it starts to stretch,
Claiming space, no need to fetch.

Neighbors stare with puzzled glee,
Is that a plant or a wild spree?
It climbs and dances, won't sit still,
Like a kid with too much wind and thrill.

It weaves and twists, a game of tag,
With little bugs on every brag.
Bright flowers laugh, watch it boast,
"Look at me, I'm the climbing toast!"

So if you spot a leafy face,
Join the fun and make some space.
For life's a race and green's the game,
Let's plant our dreams and stake our claim!

The Mysterious Ascent

One day a sprout took a brave leap,
Up the wall with a mighty peep.
It said, "I'm here to reach the sky,
And no one knows quite how or why!"

The fence looked back, grumpy and old,
"Do you really think you're bold?"
"Oh yes!" said Sprout with a cheeky frown,
"I'm higher up than your old town!"

But as it climbed, it slipped a bit,
And tangled up in a twirling fit.
With roots entangled like a shoe lace,
"Help me out, I'm losing face!"

A breeze blew by, just to tease,
"Keep going up, oh mighty green breeze!"
So up it went, despite the mess,
Funny how ambition loves to stress!

Tangle of Ambitions

A sprig decided to aim for fame,
Climbing high, it played the game.
With neighbors yelling, "Grow right here!"
But it shot up, "I'm outta here!"

Each twist and turn, it made quite a fuss,
A giant tangle, oh what a plus!
With tendrils waving like hands in cheer,
It formed a knot that brought in the deer!

"Oh dear!" said the ladybug with a laugh,
"Looks like you've turned into a staff!"
"Join the party!" was the sprout's reply,
As insects gathered, oh me, oh my!

In tangled hopes and leafy play,
Every critter found a way.
What started funny turned into a feast,
Who knew ambition could be released?

Exploring New Heights

A little vine took a daring look,
At the distant roof, like an open book.
"I'll climb that height, I just might win!"
With a grin so wide, it started to spin.

Up it went, in spirals and loops,
Avoiding grumpy gathering droops.
"I'm not just climbing, I'm looking for mates!
For those who're brave and love to create!"

But mid-climb, it caught a breeze,
"Hold on tight!" it yelled with ease.
"Adventure calls, do you hear the beat?
Let's take this thrill and make it sweet!"

So off they soared, a leafy crew,
Exploring paths where laughter grew.
From one high perch to another they'd go,
In a world of green, they stole the show!

Vines in the Breeze

A twist and a turn, what a sight,
Leaves waving hello, in morning light.
Up the fence, they tease the cat,
'Catch us if you can!' they say with a pat.

In the garden, they throw a show,
With curls and swirls, putting on a glow.
They attempt to climb the old swing set,
But it's tangled mess, a leafy duet.

With a giggle and jiggle, they reach for the sun,
Always some trouble, but oh, so much fun.
Swinging around, they tickle the bees,
Laughing together in the gentle breeze.

In the evening glow, a secret shared,
How they're creeping slowly, no one's prepared.
Hitching a ride on a sleepy snail,
They're plotting a world tour, detailed in trail!

Green Threads of Life

Stitching up laughter, they loop and they twist,
In a fabric of green, none can resist.
They climb and they crawl, what a sight to behold,
Telling grand tales that never get old.

With a wink and a giggle, they scale the old gate,
Swaying with rhythm, it's never too late.
"Onward and upward," they cheerily sing,
As the neighbor's dog barks, they do their own fling.

They wrap around posts, in a dance of delight,
Covering cracks, oh what a funny sight!
Competing with squirrels, they rise to the top,
Who knew they could be a comedy shop?

In the twilight glow, they whisper a jest,
Life's just a climb; let's enjoy it, no rest!
With a sprinkle of humor, they spread far and wide,
A blanket of laughter, nature's green pride.

Nature's Steady Climb

Step by step, they make their play,
Reaching for height, come what may.
With a wink to the sky, they plot their grand scheme,
Laughing aloud in a leafy daydream.

Creeping up walls, they throw the best bash,
A leafy confetti, come join in the smash!
Announcing their presence with giggles and grins,
Who knew green could win? What a mess of spins!

With a friendly nudge, they tickle the gate,
Whispering secrets that never abate.
"Let's climb up the shed!" they chime with a cheer,
"Who needs an invitation? Just grab a giraffe here!"

In a tangle of joy, they laugh and entwine,
As the sun sets low, their spirits align.
With roots deep in laughter, they conquer the night,
Two leaf-covered jokes, a whimsical sight.

The Dance of Persistence

They twirl and they weave, such a lively scene,
Clinging to stones, looking oh so keen.
With a shimmy and shake, they stretch for the stars,
Climbing up fences and even our cars!

In the midst of the chaos, they grin and they sway,
Trying to outsmart the wind in its play.
"Can you catch us at dinner?" they laugh in delight,
As they dance in the air, a jolly sight!

With a cling and a clamber, they spin around fast,
Turning dull gardens into a blast.
They wrap their green arms, in a hug that won't fade,
Creating a tapestry, nature's parade!

Through ups and downs, they just won't relent,
Chasing the sunshine, they never grow bent.
With a riot of colors, they sing through the night,
What a funny tale of nature's green flight!

Lattice of Green Tendrils

In the garden, a vine does play,
It sneaks up and stretches away.
With a wink and a leafy grin,
It tickles the fence, ready to win.

Twisting and turning with glee,
It whispers, "Look, I'm all you see!"
Aiming for the sun's warm kiss,
In its leafy world, it finds pure bliss.

Neighbors watch with a chuckle or two,
As the little green rascal finds its view.
Climbing higher, it takes a chance,
Leaves them laughing as it forms a dance.

With every stretch, it seems to scheme,
Master of mischief, living the dream.
An acrobat in a leafy attire,
Creating a buzz, like a green-fingered hire.

Ascent of Silent Shadows

In the twilight, a vine creeps sly,
It scales the walls with a wink and a sigh.
An artist in shades of vibrant hues,
Painting the night with its greenish clues.

Tiptoeing softly up the old stone,
A comedian where the wild winds moan.
Waving its tendrils at the moon above,
Whispering secrets to stars it loves.

With every sideward glance it takes,
You'd think it plans a million pranks and shakes.
Stealing the spotlight, it's quite the show,
A comedian in foliage, ready to glow.

Silent shadows dance to its whims,
As it grows bold, twirling on limbs.
Nature's jester in the quiet night,
Bringing laughter with every sprightly height.

Whispering Vines of Fate

Tangled tales in the summer breeze,
A bundle of giggles hiding with ease.
They stretch and stretch, in a clumsy spree,
Whispering secrets to the curious bee.

With curls that giggle, they twine and tumble,
Making the sunbeam laugh, not stumble.
A knot of mischief where stories unfold,
Each little leaf embodies pure gold.

Their dance is a riddle, quite hard to crack,
Building bridges on branches, no way to look back.
In the garden of whimsy, they take a chance,
Inviting all critters for a viney dance.

As they grasp for the clouds, it's clear to see,
They've tangled their fate, wild and free.
Leaving a trail of giggles behind,
In the laughter of nature, joy aligns.

Embrace of Nature's Reach

In a merry dash to the sunny rays,
A vine skips forth in playful ways.
Reaching out with fingers so green,
In a game of tag, it's quite the scene.

Bouncing along with a chuckle and cheer,
It bends to say, "Come closer, dear!"
Wrapping around with a snug little hug,
Making everyone feel warm and snug.

The birds take turns in its leafy embrace,
Spinning round like it's a fun race.
Sunbeams giggle as they slide through,
Nature's own party, in shades of dew.

With every twist, it crafts a new path,
Creating paths of joy and laughs.
In the heart of the garden, laughter's in reach,
As life plays on with nature's own speech.

Scramble of Life

In corners of gardens, it starts to creep,
A tangle of joy that makes you leap.
With leaves all a-twirl and stems that twist,
It's chaos with laughter; you'll get no tryst.

On walls it will climb, with such carefree flair,
Like a kid on a swing, it's light as air.
Its friends, the weeds, form a raucous crew,
Who invited them? Oh! What's a gardener to do?

It loops and it bends, quite the anarchist,
Making gardens a puzzle, it's hard to resist.
"Who needs a plan?" it seems to declare,
As it gathers more sunlight than one could bear.

So join in the fun, with a chuckle and cheer,
For laughter grows wild when problems appear.
Let's dance with the vines, let's step out of line,
For life's just a scramble, and that's just fine!

Reaching Above the Ordinary

Up walls and poles, in a jiffy it surges,
Flipping off norms, oh how it emerges!
With a grin so wide, it stretches for fun,
Like a jester in green, it outshines the sun.

It knows no bounds, it seeks every height,
With a wink and a nod, it dances in light.
The neighbors look up, eyebrows raised in surprise,
At green shenanigans climbing the skies.

Who knew such antics could cause such a buzz?
The way it sneaks up — "How does it does?"
With tendrils at work, it's a playful spree,
Going where no ordinary plant would be.

In its leafy dominion, it reigns like a king,
Making mundane walls feel like a big fling.
So when life gets dull, just look all around,
For a little green mischief, waiting to be found!

A Life Wrapped in Green

With tendrils a-wiggle and colors so bright,
It wraps up the fence as if it's a kite.
"This spot's mine!" it boasts as it curls with glee,
A life wrapped in green, oh look, can't you see?

With all of its friends, a leafy parade,
It cooks up a scheme; oh, don't be dismayed!
Like green party crashers, they spread and they roam,
Painting up gardens, they won't stay at home.

It plays peekaboo with the flowers in bloom,
Turning dull spaces into a green room.
"Let's cover this post!" it shouts with delight,
And soon, everything's snuggled in lush leafy flight.

So if your life feels a bit in the dark,
Call forth some greenery, it'll hit the mark.
For laughter and joy come wrapped up in green,
And life's just a party, if you know what I mean!

The Power of Growth

Tiny tendrils twirl in the breeze so sweet,
Claiming up spaces, with nimble feet.
They whisper "I'm here, with a wink at your door,"
On this leafy adventure, who could ask for more?

With each little inch, it giggles and chants,
"I'll climb up that ledge, just give me a chance!"
The push and the pull, it just doesn't care,
Like a determined dreamer with green tousled hair.

It tickles the fenceline, with glee in its sway,
Playing games with the sun, in a wild ballet.
With roots that are planted, it stretches up high,
Chasing the clouds, giving wings to the sky.

So next time you stumble, feeling low in a rut,
Remember this green thing, give it a strut.
For all who just grow, with a laugh and a shout,
Show us the magic of life all about!

Shadows in the Harvest Moon

In the garden, a shadow creeps,
Poking fun at the squash that sleeps.
It whispers jokes to the tomatoes bright,
Underneath the harvest moonlight.

A pumpkin chuckled, out of sync,
While the cornfields tried not to blink.
Cucumbers rolled with laughter loud,
As the night wore on, feeling proud.

The carrots danced, with joy and zest,
While mischief brewed—they were the best!
As moonbeams sparkled on leafy crews,
Even the radishes shared the snooze!

Oh, the tales these shadows will tell,
Of laughter echoing like a bell!
In the garden's heart, a celebration,
In whispers, they dream of next rotation!

Reaching for the Unattainable

Stretching high, oh little sprout,
Dreaming big with a silly shout.
"Just a few more inches, please!"
Oh, how the branches sway with ease!

But there's a bird who won't relent,
Stealing seeds, it's quite the event!
"Why reach the sun when there's a crow?
You could be dinner, just so you know!"

Leaves confound with funny faces,
As they plot and create new bases.
"Hang on tight," says the breeze,
"Life's a game of tag with trees!"

The taller ones just grin and stare,
"At least you've got guts; you're not a pear!"
With each stretch and wobble they cheer,
While giggles echo, loud and clear.

Clad in Leafy Secrets

Dressed in green, with tales to share,
Wearing secrets like they're rare.
"Who tickled you?" the daisies tease,
As breezes scatter with little ease.

In every rustle, a giggle flows,
Whispered dreams in leafy prose.
"Let's conspire!" a bold tendril says,
"Let's start a dance, in mischievous ways!"

Beneath the canopy, tales unfold,
Of tangled vines that love to scold.
"Have you seen the squirrels? They plot!"
Leaves giggled at the chaos they wrought.

Hidden pranks wrapped in green delight,
Playing games from day to night.
Oh, the secrets clad on each blade,
Joy in the shade, and mischief made!

Veils of Verdant Desires

Behind the green, there's mischief brewing,
Frolicking blooms in fun pursuing.
"Let's wear veils and sneak a peek!"
At the garden party—what a week!

Petals giggle, dressed in disguise,
As crickets croon silly lullabies.
Little shoots bend with playful grace,
Unraveling secrets, a green embrace.

"Hide the twigs, we're making a fort!
With daisies as doors, come for a tour!"
Disorder roams among the leaves,
And laughter wraps around like sleeves.

As night descends, whispers twirl,
With fanciful dreams in a leafy whirl.
Under veils, they plot and scheme,
In the garden's heart, they chase a dream!

Echoes of Hidden Growth

In a garden so neat, it starts to creep,
A green little rebel, while others just sleep.
With a wink and a twist, it dances around,
Pretending to hide, but it won't be found.

It whispers to daisies, 'Let's stretch a bit!'
While they stare in shock, it won't quit.
On fences it climbs, and up trees it sings,
Oh, the mischief and joy that a small plant brings!

As it wraps 'round the gnome with a cheeky grins,
It's definitely winning, while everyone spins.
Naughtily twisting, such a clever ruse,
Who knew leafy greens could inspire such snooze?

A comedian's touch in the glens so bright,
Turning mundane to funny, oh what a sight!
While the roses just bloom, feeling all grand,
It's climbing up high, holding life in its hand.

Secrets Among the Leaves

Underneath leafy covers, there's laughter and cheer,
The whispers of secrets, only plants can hear.
The lilac's got jokes, with stories galore,
While the basil just giggles, trying not to snore.

The oak shakes its roots, 'What's that up ahead?'
A vine full of mischief, with ideas to spread.
It twirls with the breeze, a performance each day,
Leaving daisies doubled over in playful display.

In shadows and light, it plays hide-and-seek,
With tendrils that tickle, it's no longer meek.
A sprightly cousin to flowers, it brings such glee,
Chasing off worries, as wild as can be!

So here's to the green, with its light-hearted scheme,
Creating a world that feels like a dream.
Who knew that a vine could be so much fun,
When the garden's in laughter, it's never outdone!

Vertical Journeys

A sprightly little traveler, with courage untold,
It climbs up the wall, bold and uncontrolled.
With each little twist, it reaches for stars,
Making friends with the squirrels, sharing candy bars.

It giggles with each branch, 'Is it hard to fly?'
But the robin just chuckles, 'You're giving it a try!'
Through cracks and through crevices, it boldly ascends,
While it plans its great route, making all sorts of friends.

In the garden's embrace, there's mischief afoot,
With leaves doing cartwheels, oh what a hoot!
And as bees buzz along, they join in the fun,
Creating a circus beneath the warm sun.

So let's cheer on this green in its climbing quest,
Bringing laughter and joy, oh it's simply the best!
With a wink and a wave, up it goes with a smile,
The champion of growth, making each inch worthwhile!

Nature's Tenacious Spirit

With a sprig of ambition, it starts to arise,
Almost like magic, to everyone's surprise.
It tangles with fences, and tickles the gate,
Embracing its journey, it has no debate.

In the tussle and tumble, it struts with great flair,
Challenging flowers to grow and to share.
It pokes at the weeds, saying, 'Out of my way!'
While the sunlight laughs, 'Now who'll have the last play?'

Scaling up walls with a comedic twist,
Flipping off gravity, it won't be dismissed.
Between bricks and shadows, its spirit is bright,
Daring pests to dance, it's a curious sight!

So raise a glass high to this spirited green,
In the realm of plants, it's the zaniest scene.
Whipping up joy with a nudge and a climb,
Nature shows off its humor, so truly sublime!

The Hidden Climbing Path

In the garden so spry, there's a sneaky green twist,
Every time that I turn, it's a vine-laden mist.
I tripped on a root, then a leaf stole my shoe,
It whispered, "Keep going! There's more here for you!"

With the wind as my guide, I danced with delight,
The plants had a laugh, oh what a silly sight!
They giggled and wrapped, with a flourish and flair,
Embracing my legs like they just didn't care.

Bumblebees buzzing, they joined in the fun,
Wiggling their wings in the bright warming sun.
Each step felt like magic, each twist had a grin,
This climb up my porch was a riotous win!

At the top of the fence, I let out a cheer,
Finding friends in the foliage, oh so sincere.
For life's full of giggles, like this leafy dance,
Where paths twist and turn, and we take a chance!

Vine-Crafted Destinies

Behold the green dancers, in a grand tug-of-war,
Their overlapping antics leave me craving for more.
One wraps round my elbow, another on my hat,
As I laugh at this chaos, they entangle me flat.

In the midst of their fun, I yelp with surprise,
As a branch gives a poke right between my eyes.
A clever little twirl, it says, "Join us, don't stray!"
I chuckle, "Good heavens! Guess I'm here to stay!"

They plotted a giggle, oh those clever old leaves,
Conspiring together, hiding tricks up their sleeves.
With every new twist, I swear they just grin,
Creating a ruckus as they tug on my skin.

So, if you seek journeys where laughter's the prize,
Follow runners and climbers and share in their highs.
These playful green spirits will lead you along,
To a world full of chuckles, where you truly belong!

Believers in the Light

Upward they spiral, in a glorious quest,
Dressed in robes of green, they seem so possessed.
With a wink and a nod, they shout out with glee,
"Come bask in the sun, it's a party for free!"

They twirl and they spiral, as if they could fly,
Gaining heights of humor, just like a pie in the sky.
"Watch out!" I warn, as they reach for my hair,
They giggle like kids, loving the wild air.

Each leaf has a dream, to touch the bright beam,
They gather in clusters, forming whimsical teams.
With roots wrapped in laughter, they tickle the ground,
A playful reminder that joy can be found.

So join in their romp, let your spirit take flight,
In the bliss of the day, be a believer of light.
With vines as your comrades, you'll dance through the haze,
As you share in their jokes, in a twisty green maze!

Curving Towards the Infinite

Each twist leads to giggles, like a carnival ride,
Vines curling and coiling, with nature as guide.
They hoot and they holler, as they tug me along,
In this merry parade, I just hum a light song.

A leaf flutters down, it tickles my toe,
"Oh no!" they all chant, "Don't let her go slow!"
I skip like a child, with the sun in my eyes,
In this dance of the vines, I am winning the prize.

The air filled with laughter, the petals explode,
They pull and they push, on this wild little road.
Every step that I take feels like a leap in the air,
A joyride of foliage, with nature's sweet flair.

So if you find pathways that seem quite absurd,
Remember this journey, let laughter be heard.
With curves and connections, we twirl in delight,
For a funny adventure is always in sight!

Forever Climbing Higher

In gardens green, a sneaky vine,
It tickles trees, a wobbly line.
"Watch me climb!" it sings with glee,
"I'm running late for tea, you see!"

With every twist, it hugs the pole,
It reaches high, its lofty goal.
"I'll wave to birds, oh what a show!"
The sunadmirer from down below!

Its leaves a jive, it makes a fuss,
"Stand back world, I'm coming, trust!"
With feet of roots, it won't let go,
A climbing comedian, putting on a show!

When rainclouds roar, it dons a crown,
And dances wildly, never down.
"Why sit and fret?" it laughs aloud,
Forever climbing, bold and proud!

The Language of Vines

In nature's tongue, they twist and twine,
The grape's a poet, sipping wine.
"A sonnet here, a laugh or two,"
They curl up telling tales of dew!

With whispered jokes held tight between,
The leaves flap madly, mostly green.
"Did you hear?" one leaf will giggle,
"The pumpkin's round, but my jokes wiggle!"

As frost arrives, they share a chat,
"Can't take this chill! Where's my warm hat?"
Puns flow like sap, a sticky spree,
The chattering vines, so wild and free!

In the garden's race, they swirl and slide,
With glee and laughter as their guide.
"Climb up, climb up! Let's stretch and glide!"
Who knew vines had such a fun side?

Upward Whispers

Against the wall, they scramble high,
A giggle here, a wink, oh my!
"Hey, spider! Watch the moves I make!"
They leap in humor, a vine-tastic break!

With sassy leaves in shades of green,
They share the secrets that they've seen.
"A buddy lost? Don't you fret,
I'll grow around, you'll hear from me yet!"

When shadows play in evening's glow,
They sip the stars, the night winds blow.
"Join us! Thrill in heights and dreams!"
Together they dance, or so it seems!

As morning breaks, they rise and cheer,
With each new day, they shed a tear.
"We whisper jokes, let laughter thrive!"
In the climb of life, they feel alive!

Harmony of Suspended Hope

In corners thick with dreams and dew,
They dangle low, yet reach for blue.
With vines that twirl and tails that sway,
They chuckle softly, come what may!

With slippery jokes and playful charms,
They cling to fences, secure in their arms.
But when the wind begins to tease,
They party hard, the frisky breeze!

A tug, a pull, they dance in line,
While squirrels laugh and birds recline.
"Up, up, let's race! To the sun, let's go!"
Each twist and turn, a lively show!

In perfect tune, they sway and loop,
An epic tale of leafy troop.
With every breeze, they find their way,
Suspended hope in endless play!

Climbing Through Time

Once a tiny sprout, full of glee,
Reaching for heights, what could it be?
Waving at bees and chasing the sun,
Saying, 'Just wait, this is gonna be fun!'

With every twist, it dances in style,
Grabbing old fences, it goes the extra mile.
Whispering secrets to passing clouds,
While wearing a crown made of adoring crowds.

Each time it grows, it giggles aloud,
Claiming new spots, oh, isn't it proud?
It tickles the branches, it teases the breeze,
Saying, 'I'm the queen of the green, if you please!'

In the race to the top, it won't take a nap,
Swinging through moments, it's mapping a map.
Who knew a plant could have such a blast?
Climbing through time, it's a glorious contrast!

Leafy Aspirations

In a quiet garden, with dreams so bright,
A quirky little leaf took off in flight.
Hitching a ride on a bumblebee's back,
Planning a journey, oh, what a knack!

It'll reach for the sun, say, 'Look at me shine!'
Spinning with envy, 'Cause the daisies are fine.
Climbing up trellises, it's quite the sight,
Waving to flowers, 'Hey, don't I look alright?'

While giggling at roots that are stuck in the ground,
It's plotting a route, oh, the places it's found.
Over fences and walls, it glides with some flair,
Singing, 'Who's got the moves, if not I, without care?'

In its leafy ambitions, it spreads out its arms,
Swaying in rhythm, enchanting with charms.
With dreams that are bold, and laughter that sways,
This leafy aspirant will dance through its days!

The Bond of Soil and Sky

In a world where dirt and air collide,
A sprout giggles, 'Oh, what a ride!'
Soil whispers secrets, like a close friend,
While sky shouts back, 'Together, let's bend!'

They laugh and they stretch, creating a bond,
Roots dive down deep, while the leaves respond.
It's a comedic dance, a curious play,
'Cause who knew the ground had so much to say?

Under the sun, they laugh without care,
Soaking up rays and breathing the air.
With petals that twirl, they create a scene,
'We're the dynamic duo, if you know what I mean!'

As clouds float by, they giggle and sway,
Finding joy in this weird, earthy ballet.
In soil and in sky, there's laughter anew,
Together they grow, just like me and you!

Rising in Quiet Grace

A little green sprout with a dream in its gaze,
Plans to take flight through the sun's golden rays.
With a laugh in the breeze, it stretches up tall,
Saying, 'Watch me conquer, I'm having a ball!'

The raccoons cheer and the birds sing along,
As it reaches for dreams, like a whimsical song.
'Oh, look at me rise, so calm and at ease,
Dancing through moments, like summer leaf tease!'

It bends with humor, so easy, so clever,
Chasing the clouds, oh, always in endeavor.
Quietly rising, it shows off its grace,
Finding the magic in bright open space.

In the laughter of growth, it finds its own pace,
With wiggles and giggles, a true maestro of space.
Blossoming brightly, it knows it's a blast,
Rising in quiet grace, and having a feast that lasts!

The Vertical Waltz

In a garden where antics take flight,
Lanky greens dance under sunlight.
Twisting and turning, they'll never fall,
Swaying to breezes, giving their all.

They wrap around fences, they tickle the wall,
A leafy parade that's fun for all.
With each little wiggle, they claim their stage,
Nature's own dancers, setting the page.

The neighbors all chuckle, the kids point and cheer,
As vines perform shows, not a hint of fear.
A riot of green in a jolly ballet,
Cartwheeling through summers, brightening the day.

So when you see greens on a fanciful spree,
Just know it's a party that's wild and free.
Their vertical waltz is a sight to behold,
With giggles and wiggles, their stories unfold.

Climber's Heartbeat

In the garden a creature, green and spry,
Climbs up the trunk like it's aiming for the sky.
With a wiggle and jiggle, it takes its chance,
Jumping and twirling in its leafy dance.

It's got the rhythm, a heart that beats strong,
Racing up branches, serenading the throng.
Every twist taken, a victory pose,
A glorious path that nobody knows.

Each day a new challenge, a wall to ascend,
Laughing at gravity, it knows how to bend.
Outrunning the clouds in a fit of delight,
With all of its friends, it parties each night.

So next time you see that stubborn green sprout,
Remember its journey, there's joy all about.
A climber's sweet heartbeat in nature's grand jest,
Takes life as a game, oh what a fun quest!

Nature's Steadfast Ascent

Rooted in mischief, it rises with flair,
Climbing up structures without a care.
Challenging cats to a race up the fence,
The greenery giggles, it's simply immense.

With a twirl and a twist, it leaps to the sun,
Ever so sly, just having some fun.
Turning old bricks into lively friends,
As it tickles the sky, where the sunshine blends.

From dull to vibrant, the world's in a spin,
As this sprightly green prankster paints grand with a grin.

It freestyles on arches, just laughs at the height,
Saying, "Come join the climb, it's pure delight!"

So smile at the mischief, embrace every sprout,
Watch the steady ascent and the joy it's about.
In nature's own hands, every climb a surprise,
Where laughter and greenery reach for the skies.

Veils of Verdant Growth

Beneath moonlit nights, they whisper sweet dreams,
Draped like the shenanigans flowing in streams.
Veils of green giggles entwined with delight,
Swinging from branches, a party in sight.

Curtains of laughter that move with the breeze,
Wink at the stars as they dance with such ease.
Keeking at squirrels, causing playful frays,
They charm all the critters with leafy ballets.

As morning awakes, it's a playful parade,
Nature's own jesters, a leafy charade.
They twirl up the fences, they play peek-a-boo,
With every inch gained, they say, "Look at you!"

So let out a chuckle when greens come to play,
For in every leaf there's a joke on display.
Veils of verdant growth wrapping humor so tight,
Keep watching this scene, it's pure, hilarious light.

Boundless Green

In a garden so lush, it freely sprawls,
A leafy delight scaling fences and walls.
With a wiggly dance, it hugs the facade,
Its mission? To conquer, oh how very charred!

Cheeky little sprout, oh what a spree,
Clambering high with marvelous glee.
Sticking to surfaces like a tape gone wild,
Leaving homeowners both baffled and riled.

A jumpy vine with a penchant for pranks,
Creating green shadows where nobody thanks.
It whispers to daisies, "Watch where you grow!"
A green jest of nature stealing the show.

Hiding in corners, it peeks through a space,
Like a playful kid playing hide-and-seek chase.
"Who's that?" asks the weed with a jealous glare,
"I'm the King of the Garden, if you even dare!"

Latticework of Life

On trellises perched, it swings with delight,
Wiggling and jiggling, what a silly sight!
Twisting and turning with things on its mind,
"Excuse me, dear flowers, you're all in my bind!"

The woodwork shakes at the vine's grand ambush,
Grinning and giggling, it makes quite a push.
"I'll wrap around this and curl over that,
While you two just pout in your little green chat!"

A mischievous flirt, it challenges bees,
"Why buzz on about? Join my leafy spree!"
"Let's have a dance in the summer's warm glow,
With petals and pollen putting on quite a show."

Nature's own comedian with vines on a leash,
Holding court in the garden, it never seeks peace.
"It's all in good fun!" it shouts with a laugh,
As laughter rustles through the botanical path.

Spirals of Hope

Twisting and turning, a lively parade,
Climbing up posts like it's got it made.
With a sense of humor, it breeches the tall,
Feeling quite proud like it's king of them all.

"Look at me go!" it teases the trees,
As they shake their heads in the light summer breeze.
It slips and it slides, looking so spry,
The twirling uninvited, oh my, oh my!

Sending its tendrils on wild little trips,
But surely could use a map for its skips.
"Where am I off to?" it asks, in a fluster,
While bees buzz around in a mild lil' luster.

With every twist, a chuckle survives,
Bringing us joy while it plays with our lives.
A comedian of green, in the sunlight it hops,
Ever so sly, from the bottoms to tops!

Nature's Quiet Rebellion

Tired of sitting, it enters the scene,
Sneaking and creeping, all glossy and green,
Whispering loudly, "Let's break down the fence,
Burgle the brightness of neat little vests!"

With a cheeky climb, it tiptoes unseen,
Rummaging through gardens, just like a machine.
"Time for some fun!" it leaps at the chance,
Outsmarting the flowers with a viney advance.

Just when you think it's thrown in the towel,
It spins and it grins like a mischievous owl.
Nature's shady prankster, playing it cool,
Making all plants write out tribute at school.

So if you see it, please laugh in delight,
For it tells a tale when it hugs through the night.
A rebellion so quiet, yet full of sweet cheer,
Celebrating growth with a wink and a leer!

www.ingramcontent.com/pod-product-compliance
Lightning Source LLC
Chambersburg PA
CBHW070320120526
44590CB00017B/2749